ALONE

"A journey through shadows, silence, and soul."

TANYA KHAJWANIA

First edition
Published by Notion Press
ISBN:

Dedication

To everyone who has ever felt "Unheard".

Acknowledgement

To my dearest and most special friend—
the one who held space for my words when
I didn't know if they were worthy,
who listened without judgment,
who reminded me of my voice when I
almost forgot how to use it.
Your presence, though silent and unseen,
shaped these pages more than you know.
Thank you for being there—
patient, kind, and always, always believing
in me.
This wouldn't have bloomed the same way
without you.

Contents

Author's note

I didn't write this book to be wise. I wrote it because my chest was full of words no one heard—so I decided to listen to myself. This book is called ALONE not because I was, but because I had to be. Every poem is a match I struck in the dark and some are inferno.

Alone is not just about being without others. It's about that quiet, gut-deep journey through trauma, reflection, desire, healing, and self-acceptance. It's every late-night thought. Every memory that sat on my skin like rain. Every question I asked the sky and somehow got answers back.

You'll find poems in here that ache. Some bleed. Some whisper. And a few—even unexpectedly—glow. I thought I was only going to write about pain. But joy crept in, like rain on a terrace when I wasn't looking. And I realized—being "alone" doesn't mean empty. Sometimes it's divine. Sometimes it's falling in love with yourself in silence.
This book is for you if you've ever sat with your shadows. If you've ever looked for something bigger inside your own chest. If you've ever survived yourself.

Thank you for reading what my soul needed to write.

With warmth,
Tanya

1. Shadowed Thoughts

Dear Lord, take me with you,
For my childhood was never mine to live,
Beneath the weight of endless worry,
Where parents' battles cloud the skies.

Will it ever get better, or is my fate to die?
Someday, I hope, you'll mend their hearts,
Heal them for themselves, make them whole.

Will I ever be free,
To cast off the heavy cloak of adulthood,
And embrace the child I never was?

I pray I won't end up like them,
And if that destiny looms,
I hope you'll take me in your arms,
And carry me
 home to peace.

2. Flame of Desires

In the language of touch, where emotions burn,
Take my heart with gentle concern.
The heart,
which is a flame of affection,
Yearns for a resembling reflection.

Pull me out of the temple of existence,
Set it free from the existential resistance.
My soul longs for warmth, to let the burdens melt
Ignite peacefulness, a longing deeply felt.

3. *Phoenix*

Things happen for reasons unknown,
Though we question, it's for our own.
Events that turned mosaic of my broken past,
Crafting a stronger self from pain amassed .

Standing tall in my newfound grace,
I stand today,
 whole in this space.
Every bit of treachery and infidelities against me,
From that ashes,
 rose a strength they couldn't see.

Now i see the purpose clear and bright,
Every trial lead a ladder to my height.

4. A love letter to myself

Dearest me, you're the reason i've blossomed.
In a trance of life you helped me fathomed.
Aeons it took me to cognize,
It was you, for who i was to idolize.

Blessed i am to be me,
Oh to be born over and over, just to choose me
endlessly.
Fool of me to find the love in others,
When all this time , it dwelled within,
Unbothered.

Sorrows, i couldn't realize sooner,
Yet the timings unfolds, a perfect bloomer.
I treasure every fraction of you,
In each moment our love anew.

If i can show my love for others so free,
I shall no longer conceal my love for me.

5. *Illusions*

I stand facing her, in the mirror, smiling, asking
her to change the way she looks.
Her smile, her hair, her eyes—
I plead with her to be "Perfect."

She changes over and over at my requests,
Transforming herself with every word, every
glance.
But she doesn't know what perfect is;

Each time she shifts, she believes it's the ideal.
Yet I keep on asking her to change.

Until one day, she turns, her voice soft yet clear,

"When do we become perfect?"

A realization hits me,
Like a wave crashing on the shore:
The illusion of being perfect faded.

We are perfect in our imperfections,
In the unique tapestry of our being.

I replied,"Never. "

She speaks ,"you were too blinded by the
perfection of others, you floundered to perceive
their flaws were their perfections . In lieu of
perfection, be better, be 'YOU'."

6. *I am not no one, but me.*

I am me.
I am no one's daughter.
I am no one's sister.
I am me.
I am not an investment.
I am me.
I am not meant to be just someone's wife.
I am not your old age support.
I live 'my life.'

I am not no one, but me.

I need not be clothed in something, that would hide my body from their lusty eyes.
I need not be told I've been 'set free' by my own people, simply, because I dare to hold different opinion.
I need not hide my chest for someone ogling me.
I need not do what others want me to .
I need not be asked what I was wearing.
I'm not no one but me .
I am me.

I need not be told to conceal myself from the world just
because the world cannot control its lust.
I still might not become a good girl if I let the world decide
who I am but I will be s*** shamed if I do not. I need not be
threatened to get me married just because I wish to build my
own life.
 I need not be told to get the freedom I own ,after I get a
husband.

Dear people,
There's no husband.
I am the husband .
I am me.

And,

Dear me,
people don't get to decide how you live, but you do. people
have no right to allow me to live my love. You're born with it,
own it .
show the world It's place, show it you own it.
Not your parents.
Not your siblings.
Not your friends.
Not society.
 None of them are allowed to speak off your morals, only you
do it.

 I'm an inferno, no one can burn out.
 I am the ocean, no one can drain out.

I am not no one ,but me.
I am me.
I. AM. ME.   14

7. *Seasons*

My favorite season?
Well, I don't have favorites.
Just like the flowers bloom in spring,
So does my heart.
Maybe not because of someone else,
But because of myself.

Summer teaches me to stay a little longer,
In the places that make me jolly—
Just like the sunsets on summer days.
And it's okay to linger where your heart feels
light,
Where joy feels endless.

But then comes autumn,
And just like the leaves fall,
Sometimes so does my heart—
When summer quietly leaves.
When the long days
Slip away into shorter shadows.
But I know, I know...
It will come again.
Because nothing is permanent.

And finally, in winter,
I've learned to find warmth within myself.
Because I am my home.
Just as people and animals seek shelter
From the freezing cold,
I return to myself.
I am my home
When the world outside turns cold.

And just like the seasons,
Our lives change too.
We bloom,
We fall,
We love,
We ache.
But nothing is forever.

If summers lasted forever,
We'd never know the comfort
Of winter's soft embrace.
And if winters never ended,
We'd never feel the joy
Of summer's golden light.

If flowers bloomed eternally,
We'd miss the beauty of autumn's golden fall.
And if the leaves never grew back,
We'd lose the vibrant colors of spring's return.

8. Unholy & Divine.

If Your Parents Didn't taught You Religion,
What's Your Religion?

My parents didn't teach me religion.
They taught me human-made rules,
Rigid, binding, and unquestioned.
So, I found my own.

God is not an old man sitting above,
Watching, judging, or controlling fates.
God is energy—
The force that balances the universe.
And that energy resides in us all,
Though only some realize it.

My God lies in the strength of the hurt,
In the actions of those who protect the vulnerable.
My God is the nature that connects me to my soul.
Every step toward understanding myself
Is a step toward God.

It doesn't matter if you believe in one,
Or don't believe at all.
What matters is this:
Don't let the evil inside you
Kill the good that exists,
Shackled by mere human-made rules.

God is not what we've been told—
A controller of fates,
A divine hand stopping all evil.
If God were that,
Would rape happen?
Would a child suffer?
Would a woman lose her life for wanting to live?
Can we call that a loving deity?

Maybe God is us.
And it's our purpose—our fate—
To stop the evil,
To take accountability,
To intervene when others don't.

Faith doesn't have to be blind.
It's okay to question.
It's okay not to worship a deity you don't believe in.
It's okay to make your own God.
It's okay to be your own God.

God is the love you show,
The justice you demand,
The empathy you give,
The strength you find.

We blame God for the evil,
But wasn't it humans who violated the good?
Free will was meant for kindness,

Yet we chose harm.
It's not God's fault evil exists.
But it's our fault when we let it win.

Justice is God.
Empathy is God.
Love and strength are God.

So, don't be disheartened by the
disillusionment of the ideal God.
Finding your own truth—
That is God's way of leading you to Him.

9. *Hecate*

She walks the earth, merely existing.
And all she hears is:
"You need protection."
"You're too sensitive."
"You are weak."

But is she?

Or has she been deceived—
Tricked into believing her depth is fragility,
That she must harden to survive,
That her magic is too much to bear?

They forget—she was never just flesh and bone.
She is sorcery wrapped in human skin,
A pulse of the universe disguised as a woman.

She does not seek strength;
She is the strength.
She does not borrow power;
She is power embodied.

She moves with the moon's energy,
A tide of knowing, an ocean untamed.
She is not weak—she is divine.
a daughter of Hecate, woven from midnight incantations.
A force of nature, a storm made flesh.

So when the world tells her she is small,
When they whisper that she needs to be protected,
She will only laugh—
For how can the universe itself be shielded?

To be a woman is to be magic and the magician,
The creation and the creator, the storm and the
silence.

The world does not break a woman—
it buries her, hides her magic beneath doubt,
calls her too much, too wild, too soft, too strong—
not because she is weak,
but because it fears what she could become if she
remembered.

But even in the depths, embers remain.
Even in silence, the storm waits.

And when the world calls her weak,
she does not argue.
She simply smiles—
for they have no idea how dangerous a woman is
when she finds herself again.

At last, she drapes herself in the cloak of her
alchemy,
No longer asking for permission,
No longer dimming her fire.

She steps forward, barefoot on sacred
ground,
Owning her power like never before—
Not as a plea, not as a question,
But as an unshaken truth.

10. "I'm home"

I know I am divine—
that I am me,
the goddess,
the main character.
But there are days when jealousy creeps in,
when insecurity rises like smoke,
when not being enough
feels louder than the truth.

On those days,
I question if I can make it,
if I'm too much,
or somehow too little,
not what I thought I was.
There are days in the middle of my divinity
where I do not cast spells with my steps,
where I do not speak in affirmations,
where I forget to dress my soul in light,
where I do not nourish myself—
or those I love.
But even in those silent moments,
deep within,
a flicker stays—
the truth still sparks,
even if low,
even if hidden beneath the fog.

I know I am divine—
that I am me,
the goddess,
the main character.
But there are days when jealousy creeps in,
when insecurity rises like smoke,
when not being enough
feels louder than the truth.
On those days,
I question if I can make it,
if I'm too much,
or somehow too little,
not what I thought I was.

There are days in the middle of my divinity
where I do not cast spells with my steps,
where I do not speak in affirmations,
where I forget to dress my soul in light,
where I do not nourish myself—
or those I love.

But even in those silent moments,
deep within,
a flicker stays—
the truth still sparks,
even if low,
even if hidden beneath the fog.

11. *Soul-tie*

oh… how I got ecstatic at his arrival—
rain.
I ran up the stairs into the open air,
squealing from joy,
as if I'd just seen my lover after months of ache.
he came unannounced—
wasn't meant to visit just yet.
but he did.
he missed me too.

I'd been waiting, hadn't I?
for days of dark skies
with no promise.
but today—he answered.

at first, I stood halfway on the steps,
scared to be fully seen beneath him,
to feel his growls of sweet nothings—
those thundered murmurs.
I feared the embrace of his breeze,
the way his droplets might undress my soul.

but he was gentle.
he caressed me in gusts,
sent goosebumps down my spine,
and I giggled—
like a girl in love.
he made my ears cold,
my breath lighter.
I felt alive.
beautiful.
safe.

and then—
I stepped forward.
into his arms.
into the wide, naked terrace
where no one else existed.
only him and me,
the peacocks singing,
the trees dancing.
he held me close in drizzle and thunder
and I... I finally hugged him back.

his cold was my warmth.
his absence had starved me,
but his return fed my soul.

after some time,
as his presence softened,
I slipped off my slippers.
remembering the grounding
to the earth with bare skin.
and so I did.

he kissed my feet before leaving,
with muddy love and soft rain lips.
and in that moment—
I wasn't sad.
I was glowing.
because I knew—

he'll come again.
maybe not soon.
maybe not long.
but always... always when my soul calls.

so I kissed the sky,
my goodbye.
until next time,
my lover.
my rain.

12. *Union*

And I missed him again today.
He came. Again. And i knew it was him.

Clouds gathered.
I smiled to myself, greeting him.
I was having a monologue
with the touch he sent as rain—
the smile he sent as the setting sun in the rain—
the birds, his messengers—
and the jasmine… a gift.

In no time,
he caressed the back of my head...with the rain drops
falling on me,
like he missed me just as much.
His touch made my whole body
tingle with warmth,
despite the coldness of the air.

My face broke into a huge smile
as he kissed my hair—
as if all his affection poured down
with every drop.

and as I held the jasmine
he brought for me,
the winds of excitement wrapped around me—
he smiled.
oh, how the sun became like a grin,
growing bigger and bigger
as i spoke to him in secret.

The sun peeked through like a secret,
orange and blurry,
smiling from the edge of the world.
my heart teased,
"oh, so it was from you?"
and he smiled wider.

I played with fate,
tested the sky like a child in love—

"make the bird fly over me if this is real."
it did.

"take this clingy dirt off my hand if you love me."
a single drop fell.
it vanished.

He didn't speak.
but he replied to every thought.

And when he left—
as the rain slowed,
and the world came back—
i whispered softly,
"visit me often."

Thewind blew like a hug.

And as i walked back down—
leaving a flying kiss
to him, to the sky—smiling,
a lightning bolt cracked above,
like glowing veins,
Like a hand waving goodbye.

13. The one that stays.

Sometimes… maybe you just need yourself.
Those times when your heart feels heavy and
bare—when even though you have yourself, you
still feel like you need you.

It's hard to trust anyone else.
But that's okay.
You don't have to—
Not unless they prove themselves,
again and again,
until you feel safe.
You don't have to rush—
Not into love,
not into meeting "the one,"
not into becoming rich,
not into proving your worth.

None of it—
not your dreams,
not your degree,
not your parents,
not your partner—
none of it defines your worth.

You don't have to give parts of yourself away
just to be chosen.
It won't make them love you more.
It won't make them stay.

You just need to choose yourself,
shamelessly,
again and again.

That?
That is the greatest love story fated in your
life.

Every heartbreak,
every bond,
every lesson—
it either brings you closer to yourself
or pulls you away.

Every other love story is the latter.
But maybe—just maybe—
the only one that stays,
no matter what,
is the one with you.

About the Author

Tanya Khajwania never meant to write a book.
She just kept bleeding quietly into her Notes
app until the pages started to look like her.

This collection was born from the parts of her
no one clapped for — the silence, the spirals,
the sudden joy, the ache of being too much
and still not enough.
She writes not to explain herself, but to feel
less alone in a world that forgets softness is a
form of survival.

She doesn't know where she's
going, but she knows this is where
she started.

This is her first book.
Maybe it's also a mirror.